EX LIBRIS

Name ______________________

Address ______________________

____

____

Telephone ______________________

Fax ______________________

e-mail ______________________

Text

Natalidita Ningthoukhongjam
&
Ashwini S. George

ISBN: 978-93-5036-852-7

Kalabindu Enterprises P. Ltd.
GF–18, Virat Bhawan
Commercial Complex, Mukherjee Nagar
Delhi 110009
Phone: +91-11-47038000

Celebrating Childhood in English Fiction

Harry Potter with the Golden Snitch

A NOTEBOOK

Introduction

"Children see magic because they look for it."
— Christopher Moore

Stories are a part of our childhood, whether they are Grimm's Fairy Tales, Aesop's Fables, the Panchatantra, or local folklore. Stories offer new worlds full of strange and wonderful possibilities; they instil the spirit of imagination and invention in the flexible impressionable minds of the reader.

Stories about children are therefore molded by these very qualities. As children we meet fantastical creatures and experience exciting exploits. We read about heroes who are our age and are brave, courageous and upright. As we grow older, though the distance between us and these stories increases, they never leave our consciousness. We return to them, nostalgic for a period in our life when the world was simple and more thrilling.

There are uncountable characters from literature and fiction whose names we can recite offhand. Alice, Huck, Aladdin, Peter, Mowgli, Heidi, Dorothy, Oliver, William, Swami, Rusty, Harry, Lucy, the Little Prince and the children from the universe of comics, are just a few of the more famous ones that we have included in this charmed

circle. From different eras and based in different regions they have gently carved their own niches in our hearts.

Some of these children have become idioms and metaphors.

"She had an Alice-like quality about her."

"You are such a Peter Pan. You will never grow up."

The word 'wizard' has become synonymous with Harry Potter and Mowgli is the standard for children of the wild. Oliver Twist is a powerful symbol of the Industrial Revolution when children of the street were abused and exploited. Through Swami we get a glimpse of Indian boys growing up in pre-Independence India, trapped between western education and the dawning awareness of native identity.

These children of literature, like the child in us, dwell in the twilight zone of consciousness. As Tinkerbell says to Peter Pan, "You know that place between sleep and awake, the place where you can still remember dreaming? That's where I'll always love you. That's where I'll be waiting."

Aladdin

"You're only in trouble if you get caught."

Popularized by Disney Aladdin, has become a household name. The Arabian boy's rags-to-riches tale is a prominent part of today's culture. Which child wouldn't want to be Aladdin and hang out with his friends—Abu the monkey, the flying carpet and the Genie? Who wouldn't envy him for winning the heart of the clever and beautiful Princess Jasmine? And who wouldn't warm up to Aladdin—plucky, clever and romantic that he is?

This version of Aladdin that we know, with his purple vest and white trousers, was rewritten by Disney to fit modern sensibilities. The original Aladdin from the *Arabian Nights* is different in many respects. He is cunning, manipulative, ambitious and has no qualms about killing. He is also less romantic; instead of wooing the princess, he abducts her so that she is separated from her rightful husband. The genie is no friend of his. Their relationship is clearly shown to follow a master-slave pattern, with Aladdin summoning the genie only to fulfill his demands.

Modern readers might not have been a fan of this Aladdin, but the basic plot is one that we find irresistible. Aladdin is a success story. Born into poverty, he discovers miraculous powers through a lamp and a ring, both of which house genies. These powers help him obtain whatever he wants. Even when they are taken away from him, he uses his wit and determination to defeat evil wizards, win the princess back, and bring about a happy end. He is definitely a hero in his own right.

"Ask not, but eat," replied Aladdin.
So they sat at breakfast till it was dinner time and Aladdin told his mother about the lamp. She begged him to sell it and have nothing to do with devils.
"No," said Aladdin, "since chance hath made us aware of its virtues, we will use it and the ring likewise, which I shall always wear on my finger."

Oliver Twist

"Please, sir, I want some more."

The figure of the orphan is a recurrent symbol in literature and has been frequently used in contemporary works of fiction. Removed from parental care and support, the orphan exists as an easy target for evil forces and thus becomes the perfect image of the hero. But before Harry Potter, before Bruce Wayne/Batman and Peter Parker/Spider Man, before even Huckleberry Finn, there was Oliver Twist, the boy who survived all odds.

Oliver Twist is the titular character of one of Charles Dickens's most memorable novels, *Oliver Twist; or, The Parish Boy's Progress* (1837–1839). Dickens, who personally experienced the extreme hardships of an impoverished life as a child, was a passionate critique of the Age's abuse of poor children living on the street—how they were mistreated as orphans and laborers, and how they were inducted into a life of crime. Oliver faces all of these evils; he is ill-treated at the workhouse, ill-treated by the wife of a man who took him as an apprentice, and bullied and pursued by the minions of Fagin, a criminal who recruits street children and turns them into thieves.

Oliver's inherent goodness and innocence continually save him. The quote above is a famous line spoken by Oliver. Hungry and unaware of the cruelty at the workhouse, the young boy asks for more gruel and is severely punished for it. This purity of soul serves Oliver well in the end as he not only escapes the clutches of Fagin and his own wicked half-brother, Monks, but manages to win the sympathy of kinder people like Mr. Brownlow, the judge and Nancy, the prostitute. He reunites with his lost aunt at last and lives happily thereafter.

"... think how young he is, think that he may never have known a mother's love, or the comfort of a home; and that ill-usage and blows, or the want of bread, may have driven him to herd with men who have forced him to guilt."

Alice

"I can't go back to yesterday because I was a different person then."

When Lewis Carroll's *Alice's Adventures in Wonderland* first came out in 1865, readers and critics were baffled. The book appeared to be full of nonsense. Its plot consisted solely of fantastical adventures that the curious seven-year-old Alice has in a place called Wonderland. When the second book, *Through the Looking Glass,* was published, Carroll's work gained the appreciation it deserved. Alice became a popular character of children's literature—a position she holds till date.

Alice's adventures in the two books still defy logic, but they are special precisely for that reason. She is an immensely curious, confident and independent child, and the pages of the book are fed by these defining characteristics. Her thirst for knowledge and keen imagination, mirror the accommodating mind of the young.

Alice is also a product of the Victorian Era, when children from affluent families grew up mostly under the care of nannies. She is therefore detached from her parents, and at the same time, protected by the manners and education she has leared by rote. This self-assurance is put to test in Wonderland that comes with its own set of mad rules and ethics. Clashes occur between the opposing values of the two worlds and Alice is forced to revise her learning to survive in Wonderland.

As symptomatic as these clashes are of the Victorian era's general fear of disorder, Alice's adventures are not read for the sake of their historical context. Alice endures because, by virtue of her ignorance and innocence, she allows the reader to enjoy and analyze the strange logic of Wonderland. Her experiences offer us a window into the extraordinary imaginations we entertained at an age when much seemed possible.

"Curiouser and curiouser!" cried Alice (she was so much surprised, that for the moment she quite forgot how to speak good English); "now I'm opening out like the largest telescope that ever was! Goodbye, feet!"

34

Heidi

"I'll always say my prayers... and if God doesn't answer them at once I shall know it's because He's planning something better for me."

Childhood is that stage when we consider life as endowed with simpler, yet forceful values. A child with her innocence, faith and love, can move the hardest of hearts. Armed with such disarming attributes, Johanna Spyri's Adelheid unconsciously weaves magic on those whom she meets. She influences them to become better human beings and brings happiness into their lives.

Spyri's *Heidi* was published in 1880, a time when industrialization had changed the old social order and introduced a spirit of fear and uncertainty in the minds of the people. Many were displaced and forced to migrate to cities and towns—places whose culture and codes were alien and alienating. Spyri paints Heidi's character against this background, making her a symbol of the negotiation between this new world and the old.

In the Swiss Alps, Heidi brings fulfillment to those with whom she comes in contact. She may be a five-year-old orphan living with the brusque and reclusive grandfather, Alm Uncle, but she makes friends and reads to Peter's blind grandmother as well. Even Alm Uncle thaws toward her and is persuaded to come out of his semi-exile. Heidi is closely tied to nature and the rustic way of life; when she goes to the city, her health deteriorates. It is when she returns to the Alps that she regains her lost carefree self.

Spyri however does not restrict Heidi to one end of the spectrum—she successfully makes a friend, Clara, in the city. When Clara visits the Alps, Heidi takes care of her till she is able to walk again. Heidi is thus representative of a bridge between differing values, a bridge that is made possible by her goodness and unchanging trust in God and humanity.

"Oh, I have the same dream every night. I always think I am with my grandfather again and can hear the fir trees roar. I always think how beautiful the stars must be, and then I open the door of the hut, and oh, it is so wonderful!"

Huckleberry Finn

"All right, then, I'll go to hell."

Mark Twain's *The Adventures of Huckleberry Finn* created a storm when it was first published in 1884, and it remains a controversial book to date. Many critics disliked it for its racist undertones while others weren't keen on the depiction of wayward children. But there have been others who interpret the novel as a challenge against racism—a challenge made possible through the character of Huckleberry Finn, the teenaged hero of the story.

Huck Finn, a smart, courageous and adventurous boy, comes from the poorer section of white society. Neglected by his drunkard father and ignorant of etiquette, he is distanced from the accepted social codes of his time. This makes Huck different from other kids; his perspective on life is self-made, and he constantly suffers from ethical dilemmas. For instance, he stays with his abusive father out of a sense of duty, but ditches the same man out of necessity.

Huck's relationship with Jim, the black runaway, is the highlight of the book and also the most significant factor in the anti-racism argument. A part of him believes the misconception that blacks are naturally inferior to whites. Ultimately he begins to appreciate Jim as a person, and therefore declares that if helping Jim sends him to hell, he *will* go to hell.

The moral crisis regarding Jim brings out the best in Huck; it shows that Huck, unlike most Americans of his time, judges people with his heart. He may not be a perfect human being yet—after all, he steals, lies and cheats people in order to survive—but he can think for himself and identify right from wrong. Though he may be unschooled in 'manners,' his innate goodness makes him a good friend and an even better person.

"We said there wasn't no home like a raft, after all. Other places do seem so cramped up and smothery, but a raft don't. You feel mighty free and easy and comfortable on a raft."

Mowgli

"I will remember what I was, I am sick of rope and chains—
I will remember my old strength and all my forest affairs."

In fiction as well as in reality, the feral child is a child brought up by animals, far away from human influence. Mowgli is arguably the most renowned example of the fictional variety. In fact Kipling's beloved character from *The Jungle Book* (1894) greatly influenced the imagination of others, such as Edgar Rice Burrough.

Mowgli is brought up in the jungle by a wolf pack. He grows into a life governed by discipline, action and loyalty. Like his wolf brothers, he can hunt and fight; unlike them, he has fingers that he can use to remove thorns from the paws of animals. Mowgli thus represents the best of both the animal and the human world.

Through Mowgli's adventures with the animals, Kipling depicts a culture that is in many ways comparable to ours. There is friendship, but there is also enmity. For friends, Mowgli has Bagheera the black panther, Kaa the python and Baloo the bear, amongst others. In Shere Khan, the ferocious tiger, he faces a deadly enemy. However the main philosophical preoccupation of Mowgli's existence is this—is he a wolf, or is he human?

Mowgli is given the chance to mingle with both humans and animals. He learns to adapt to both ways of life. When he chooses his adoptive parents, he reminds us that the call of our true nature and identity cannot be denied; when he still retains his relationship with his wolf brothers, he teaches us that we do not have to forsake our friends to live our identity. He is thus both wolf and human—a person loyal to his roots.

"I have the Pack and I have thee; and Baloo, though he is so lazy, might strike a blow or two for my sake. Why should I be afraid?"

Dorothy Gale

"If we walk far enough, we shall sometime come to someplace."

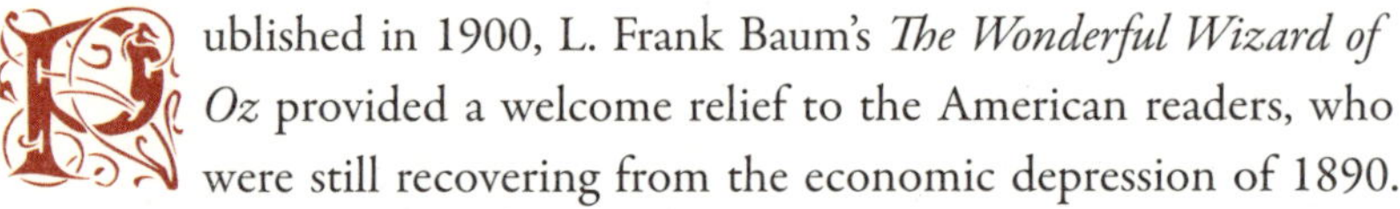

Published in 1900, L. Frank Baum's *The Wonderful Wizard of Oz* provided a welcome relief to the American readers, who were still recovering from the economic depression of 1890. Dorothy Gale, an orphan from the laboring class population of Kansas, and her dog, Toto, are swept off by a tornado and deposited in the world of Oz. There they encounter flying monkeys, china princesses and witches, both good and bad, and together with new friends, they fight evil forces and go on quests till Dorothy can find a way back home.

Dorothy is a wholesome girl who possesses all the traits and values that Americans in general favor. She is pragmatic; instead of questioning the possibility of Oz's existence, she adapts herself to it and proceeds to navigate her way through it. The meetings with the Tin Woodman, the Scarecrow, the Cowardly Lion, or the China Princess, do not perturb her, as unreal as they seem. Her unspoken motto is to spot the problem and fix it, and by the time she leaves Oz, she has defeated wicked witches, helped her friends become rulers of kingdoms, and restored peace and order.

Dorothy also gains favorable points for her humility and purity. Her one goal is to return to her uncle and aunt in Kansas. She is unblemished by her time in Oz. There is no nagging desire to go back to a land where the marvelous is possible. Such strength of character makes her suitable to play the role of the resolute hero; she acts not out of selfish ambition, but solely from the honorable need to set things right again.

"If I ever go looking for my heart's desire again, I won't look any further than my own backyard. Because if it isn't there, I never really lost it to begin with."

Peter Pan

"To die would be an awfully big adventure."

With his elf-like ears, green tunic and tights and red hair, J. M. Barrie's Peter Pan is one of the most recognizable figures from fiction. He first appeared in Barrie's 1902 novel, *The Little White Bird*, and since then has been portrayed in various stage and cinematic adaptations as a mischievous yet endearing boy.

Peter Pan is a combination of several common human desires—eternal life, supernatural power and access to a fantasy land where unusual and magical things exist. Also known as 'The Boy Who Wouldn't Grow up,' Peter is frozen in a perpetual state of childhood. He can fly, as well as teach other children to fly, and he lives in the island of Neverland, where mermaids, fairies and pirates can be found. He is full of daring, arrogance and cunning. Nevertheless, Peter is loyal to his friends, the Lost Boys and Wendy, and he goes to great lengths to save them from harm.

If one considers the historical context of J. M. Barrie's creation, Peter becomes a realization of the wish to escape from the Victorian tradition of propriety and on a more universal level, the child's yearning to gain freedom from restrictions. Yet in some respects, he may also be seen as a tragic figure. Peter can never escape childhood; his experiences are often removed from his memory so that he may remain innocent.

Reckless though he may be, Peter Pan's character raises deep philosophical questions. If one must gain the benefits of unending youth, should one have to sacrifice knowledge of the human way of life? For Peter, only 'Neverland' can bestow him his identity, and so he turns to it for his momentary escape.

"You see, Wendy, when the first baby laughed for the first time, its laugh broke into a thousand pieces and they all went skipping about and that was the beginning of fairies."

66

68

William Brown

"I never meant to do it!"

Taking after Mark Twain's Tom Sawyer, Richmal Crompton's William Brown is a roguish and inquisitive boy, who thrives on boyish exploits carried out with his gang, the Outlaws. Unlike Tom, who can be purposefully unkind at times, William believes in helping others. Yet every time he tries to help someone, the mission ends with consequences that are catastrophic for the characters, but hilarious for the readers.

William Brown is an eleven-year-old schoolboy. He lives with his parents and two older siblings, all of whom have a difficult relationship with him. They suffer continually on account of William's meddling in their affairs, as well as in the affairs of others. Sadly each setback only spurs William forward.

William's well-meaning intentions are what make his unfortunate escapades a treat to read. Often after a venture has failed, he defends himself with the argument that he never meant to do it, which is less a lie and more an eagerness to explain his honest intent. This routine raises the comedic value of the William books and explains why they don't lose their impact, even though they are set in various eras in the history of the twentieth century.

Having worked as a school mistress, Richmal Crompton certainly knew how to write about boys. William is the very definition of a young boy—dismissive of girls, hungry for adventure, allergic to personal hygiene and desirous of shouldering adult responsibilities, without really knowing how to go about it. Although the books have diminished in popularity, they still provide entertainment for readers looking for a quick laugh, because William is just that funny and engaging.

"The sort of things I want to do they don't want me to do an' the sort of things I don't want to do they want me to do."

Swami

"If one has got to read even during holidays, I don't see why holidays are given at all?"

Swaminathan (Swami) is one of the most beloved characters from the world of R. K. Narayan's Malgudi. He is a ten-year-old boy, who lives on Vinayak Mudali Street with his family, in an era when the resistance against the British Raj was in full swing. The stories of his adventures (and misadventures) with his friends Somu, Sankar, Pea, Mani and Rajam, are told in *Swami and Friends* (1935).

Fearful of his strict father and wary of his smarter friends' cunning, Swami is eager to establish his own authority and identity. Swami's tales exemplify the delightful trials of childhood where innocent ideals clash with reality. Though he often seeks refuge in his grandmother's company, Swami strives to be seen as an adult. He tries to solve his problems on his own, rather than approach his elders. One of his proudest achievements is the establishment of the MCC (Malgudi Cricket Club) that he founds with his friends. At the same time, nothing gives him greater pleasure than vacations. In one chapter, he goes to great lengths to obtain a hoop, a pursuit that Narayan describes as a 'consuming passion.'

The combination of childish desires with adult goals is written with a wonderful blend of humor and seriousness. In Swami we see a reflection of our own childhood. Immature as his struggles are when compared to problems faced by grown-ups, they create in us a longing to return to a time characterized by naive flights of fancy and the unawareness of limitations.

"I will tell you the truth, doctor. I have to play a match next week against the Young Men's Union. And I must have some practice. And yet every evening there is Drill Class, Scouting, some dirty period or other. If you could give me a certificate asking them to let me off at four-thirty, it would help the MCC to win the match."

Richie Rich & Gang

"I didn't know you had an art studio in your home! Thanks for letting me use it Richie."
"You're welcome Dot. Say... what a lot of dot pictures you've made."
"I love drawing dots! I could go on drawing dots all day!"

America experienced a huge baby boom after World War II ended. It was a time of hope and an era of rebuilding a new cultural landscape. Harvey Comics helped fill the vacuum with their riot of lively child characters and their business did exceedingly well in the 1960s. Though the appeal of the comics declined in the later decades of the twentieth century, many of these characters hold a special place in the hearts of those who grew up with them.

Richie Rich, Little Lotta, Little Dot, Casper the Friendly Ghost, Wendy the Good Little Witch, Hot Stuff the Little Devil and Baby Huey are some of the best-known characters. All of them are little children with distinct personalities. Richie Rich is outrageously wealthy yet generous, Little Lotta has a passion for food and is immensely strong, Little Dot is fascinated with dots, Casper is a warm and loving ghost and so on.

What set the Harvey characters apart from contemporary comic-book characters, was their unexpected progressiveness. They overturned popular conceptions—with Casper, they made the scary friendly; with Little Lotta, they had a girl exhibiting superhuman strength; with Little Dot and Little Audrey, they invented female characters who were into baseball, a predominately male sport in the conservative era. Although dated in their format, the comics of Harvey thus suit the comparatively liberal spirit of our time and can be easily read and enjoyed by the children of today.

"Now...if my idea about diamond bearings works, I am going to have one fast skateboard! With a model like this I will never be skatebored!"

The Little Prince

"Only the children know what they are looking for."

The Little Prince or *Le Petit Prince*, as it is known in French, is a tribute to the expansive outlook of childhood and a critique of the dull rationalism of adulthood. The narrator crashes his plane into a desert and meets a nameless boy, simply referred to as 'The Little Prince,' who has come to explore Earth.

The fact that the Little Prince is an outsider, as well as a young boy on a mission to travel to different worlds, makes him an impartial observer of life on Earth. He is unafraid of risks and unafraid to discuss his emotions and feelings. The Little Prince is quite open when it comes to talking to the narrator about his own history; he readily tells the narrator about his attachment to the rose and the wisdom he gained from the fox. The latter however treasures him for an important reason—only the Little Prince can correctly identify the subjects of the narrator's inventive drawings. While everybody else sees a hat in the narrator's Drawing Number One, the Little Prince recognizes it as the picture of a boa constrictor eating an elephant!

Like Lewis Carroll's Alice or C. S. Lewis's Lucy, the unrestrained imagination of the Little Prince connects him to what is wondrous. He is more receptive of his environment and is thus quicker to appreciate the worth of something. This attitude was intentional on the part of the author, Antoine de Saint-Exupéry. Having fled his country, France, to avoid Nazi persecution, Saint-Exupéry wrote his seminal work while grappling with a great deal of disillusionment. The Little Prince is symbolic of his wish for a better humanity—one that is kinder, more compassionate, and more progressive.

"I wonder," he said, "whether the stars are set alight in heaven so that one day each one of us may find his own again.... Look at my planet. It is right there above us. But how far away it is!"

Lucy Pevensie

"I think—I don't know—but I think I could be brave enough."

Chronicles of Narnia, C. S. Lewis's masterpiece, begins with the World War II. The Blitzkrieg has started. To escape the German air raids, the Pevensie children are sent off to the countryside, where they are to live with Professor Digory Kirke. In a time of fear, the professor's house provides a safe refuge for them, but they are shut up in its premises. When Lucy reveals her discovery of Narnia, a magical land of never-ending winter that she has accessed through a wardrobe, is she telling the truth? Or is it the overactive imagination of a child talking—a child dealing with the trauma of war, no less?

Being just eight years old, she has the most pliable mind, but it is not for this reason that Lucy is chosen to discover Narnia. Of the four siblings, she has the greatest faith and the biggest heart. She easily believes in Narnia and accepts the existence of fauns and talking beavers because she trusts more readily than the others. As a result, she is the closest to Aslan, the Christ figure of Lewis's fictional world.

In Lucy we find all the makings of a heroine, whose courage strengthens and generosity increases as the books progress. Her weakness—the desire to look as attractive as her older sister, Susan—is exposed and eliminated since Lucy is beautiful without physical appeal. The title bestowed upon her by Aslan, 'Lucy the Valiant,' does justice to her admirable character.

Unsurprisingly it is Lucy who never loses the tie with Narnia. There is a lesson to be learnt here—by remaining pure and good, we will stay connected to what is eternal.

"I see," she said. "This is still Narnia, and more real and more beautiful than the Narnia down below, just as *it* was more real and beautiful outside the Stable door! I see...world within world, Narnia within Narnia..."

107

Rusty

*"If Granny was the best cook in the world,
I must have been the boy with the best appetite."*

Ruskin Bond is one of India's best known and most prolific writers. As an Anglo-Indian growing up in various cities of India, he had an unusual childhood. After his father's death in 1944, Bond was raised by his grandmother in Dehradun. When he wrote his first novel, *The Room on the Roof*, at the age of seventeen, he wove semi-autobiographical elements into it and based the protagonist on his childhood self. This character, Rusty, would eventually feature in several novels for children, such as *Delhi Is Not Far, Rusty Runs Away,* and *Rusty, the Boy From the Hills.*

What makes Rusty an interesting character is not only that there are glimpses of Bond's presence in him, but also the fact that he makes up a part of the socio-historical context of the stories. Rusty is an Anglo-Indian orphan living in pre-Independence India. Through his eyes, the reader learns about contemporary racial discrimination, such as the existence of separate bazaars for Anglo-Indians. The rebellious and brave Rusty sneaks into the Indian bazaar and starts building a network of friends.

Rusty's adventurous spirit is the soul of Bond's books. Whether it is feuding with animals, going on a road-trip with his friends, fleeing from war-torn Java, bonding with a lonely princess, or engaging in a battle of wits with his rival, the lazy Uncle Ken, his experiences are brightened by his fearlessness, sense of humor, and willingness to take risks. Rusty is, in many ways, the fitting picture of an adolescent trying to make the most of every moment. It is no wonder then that he remains Bond's most memorable character.

"But the trees seemed to know me. They whispered among themselves and beckoned me nearer. And looking around, I noticed that other small trees and wild plants and grasses had sprung up under the protection of the trees we had placed there."

Harry Potter

"I'm going to keep going until I succeed—or die. Don't think I don't know how this might end. I've known it for years."

According to J. K. Rowling, Harry Potter simply walked into her head during a train journey. She wrote down her idea on a napkin. When the books were finally published, her life, as well as those of her millions of readers, dramatically changed; for Harry's story touches our innermost desires and deepest fears.

Rowling's success in creating the most famous child-hero of the last fifty years lies not only in the fascinating spells and enchantments of Harry's world, or his epic confrontation with Lord Voldemort. It is Harry himself who is irresistible. As an ill-treated child destined for bigger things, he arouses our interest. As an eleven-year-old discovering his phenomenal powers, he appeals to our own wish for extraordinariness. But as a loyal friend, as a modest, brave and funny boy, he is one of us, and wins our heart. Though a kid wizard, he is never far from the real child—his magic is not the product of esoteric knowledge; it channels through his own insecurities, fears and weaknesses, becoming effective only when he has overcome them. The story thus evolves from a simple tale of good versus evil to one that is made complex and profound by its study of human character, the interplay of human relationships and the plurality of choices.

Above all it is Harry's distaste for discrimination that makes him such a great role model. To Harry, Muggles, Muggle-borns, Half-bloods and Pure-blood wizards, are all equal. In a world where racial prejudice still persists, his spirited love for humanity and keen sense of right and wrong are important attitudes to emulate. His story is not only to be absorbed, digested and treasured.

"Yeh could've died!" sobbed Hagrid. "An' don' say the name!"

"VOLDEMORT!" Harry bellowed, and Hagrid was so shocked, he stopped crying. "I've met him and I'm calling him by his name. Please cheer up, Hagrid, we saved the Stone, it's gone, he can't use it. Have a Chocolate Frog, I've got loads...!"

123

ACKNOWLEDGEMENTS

PHOTO CREDITS

Cover	James Mahoney/Wikimedia Commons
Page 6 (bottom)	W.W. Denslow/Wikimedia Commons
Page 7 (center)	E.W. Kemble/Wikimedia Commons
Page 7 (bottom)	Maciej Sojka/Shutterstock.com
Page 22	Joseph Clayton Clarke/Wikimedia Commons
Page 23	James Mahoney/Wikimedia Commons
Page 31	Arthur Rackham/Wikimedia Commons
Page 38	Jessie Willcox Smith/Wikimedia Commons
Page 39	Jessie Willcox Smith/Wikimedia Commons
Page 44	E.W. Kemble/Wikimedia Commons
Page 45	E.W. Kemble/Wikimedia Commons
Page 56	W.W. Denslow/Wikimedia Commons
Page 57	W.W. Denslow/Wikimedia Commons
Page 63 (background)	Wikimedia Commons
Page 94	Denmorgan/Shutterstock.com
Page 95	Hasselnott/Shutterstock.com
Frontpaper & Endpaper	James Mahoney/Wikimedia Commons

Celebrating Childhood in English Fiction

Note: The contents are listed in the order of their date of publication.